What I Heard from a Star

Laura Orvieto

We are free, immortal souls. It's time to be happy.

I dedicate this book to my grandma, Abuelita Maria. I love you with all my heart.

Table of Contents

Introduction

My first two books were born at less than felicitous times in my life. With the book of poems "Huellas en la arena" (Footprints in the Sand) my daughter Danyella was very ill and I had to quit my job in order to rediscover my passion for writing. With "Espejismos de un mundo irreal" (Mirages of an Unreal World), all the socio-economic situations afflicting us at that time in the world and that unfortunately are still part of our collective reality, such as suicide, immigration and the like, were causing me deep pain. This was reflected in the short stories in my book.

Unlike the previous ones, this new book came about during the best time of my life. It came into being when I accepted myself, remembered myself, when I let myself be. I'm still aware of the social problems surrounding me, but I no longer feel any pain, only light, love and an immense need to heal.

When I was a little girl, I thought I was going to be a doctor because I didn't like to see people sick or sad. I tried all sorts of ways to make people laugh; I tried to look on the bright side, even in difficult situations. Later on, I discovered my vocation as a healer, with words, with a look, even though I haven't dedicated myself to medicine, I always knew that healing was my thing.

My adolescence was a little difficult, I always felt too strongly, I always saw too much, and this caused me to feel sad and alienated from my surroundings more than once. I could never understand violence, selfishness or indifference. For me the leaves on the trees didn't fall, they danced. For me the night was not dark, it was a party, and I really enjoyed sitting for hours in the courtyard of my house in Ecuador admiring the stars, so much so that I think we became friends. I remember as a child I used to love to look at the sky, look for shooting stars and talk to the moon. One night, while gazing into the heavens, I saw a white dove fly across the sky. I was particularly impressed by its color and the golden cross in its beak, so I ran to tell my grandma. I asked her what she thought it might mean, and she said: "It's the Holy Spirit, Laurita." I ran out happily to thank heaven for such a beautiful sign. I actually felt that by looking up so much, I had made more friends in heaven than on earth. For me every star, every dove, every cloud was an answer to a prayer, and I prayed often. More than once an aunt or uncle of mine would be startled to see a little girl no more than six, on her knees facing the sun, but "that's the way I was." I remember my grandma would laughingly say, "That's the way she is."

Another saying I always remember from my grandma is "If you're sick and still eat, you'll get back on your feet." She'd remind me of that as she watched me devour my food—even with a high fever—hinting that I was almost immortal because she'd never seen me without an appetite. She always made me laugh! I'm sure I inherited my sense of humor from her, among many other things. My grandma was a very important part of my childhood. She was the one who taught me to love and respect nature. I liked to see how she watered her plants so lovingly, and she always reminded me that they were medicinal. I remember her making big pitchers of horsetail and plantain tea. It was from her that I learned the importance of humility, to keep my feet on the ground no matter what material goods I might possess or how far I might get in life, to always be at the service of others and never lose faith.

As time passes I come closer to her teachings, to the infinite love I feel for nature and to fill my soul with those simple memories from my childhood, which make up the human being I am today, and the great legacy that will be my books. "What I Heard from a Star" is an account of all the beautiful things I've learned over the years to be happy being "the way I am." You may ask, "What is it like to be like that?" but I have a feeling that if you have this book in your hands you may already be "like that," the same as me, or you may know someone who is "like that," and that's why we've met.

"That way" is how it is for everyone who can't tolerate injustice, who feels sad when they see someone else suffer, even if they don't know them, who has strong feelings, who might have a premonition when something is going to happen, who can feel it in their gut when someone is not truly good; they show all their teeth when they're happy. When they love, when they love all the way, and when they're betrayed or disappointed, they feel like they could die. That's the way we are, we feel everything with every fiber of our being.

Through this book I invite you to a very important journey, the journey into your own being. We'll make friends with your sorrows and multiply your joys even more.

Welcome to "What I Heard from a Star." I'd like to think that, more than a book, this is a boat in which we shall set sail from one shore and travel together to a place where we'll be the best version of ourselves.

"What I Heard From a Star" is a book that aims at showing you the tools you need not only to find your inner strength, but also to learn how to feed, clean and strengthen it so that you no longer need external sources to be happy. You were born with everything you need to make your dreams come true and stay in harmony with the universe. The journey through life need not be a difficult and tortuous one. The time has come for you to enjoy every moment and feel that this is the best adventure of them all—your life! It doesn't matter if things outside you are out of order. How are your thoughts doing? How's your heart? If you're doing everything right, why aren't you completely happy? Do you feel frustrated and imprisoned in your own life?

That's not necessary, none of that is necessary. Breathe, feel the power, feel the energy. Are you ready? Let's embark on that journey together! Thank you for "being that way."

Questions and Answers

Who is this book for?

This book is addressed to people who feel more strongly than most, who are affected by the suffering of others, as if it were their own, who are concerned about their social environment and the future of the planet. For those who at some point have felt segregated because the bad vibes of a place affect them, and they couldn't explain why.

What can you expect from the book?

This book was written to be practical and casual. It offers you a space for a personal diary, where you can keep track of your progress and questions. As such, this book will be a journey into your inner self, and I hope you'll find in it the inspiration, the answers and the light that I found in writing it.

Who is this book not for?

This book is not for grumps who criticize books that try to inspire or motivate. It's not for people who think they're experts on everything that's ever happened. This book was written by and for sensitive souls, their inner healing and discovery so they can flourish as spiritual beings living in a physical body.

How do I read it?

The book is divided into 10 chapters. You can read them in order, or you can work on the chapters that catch your eye. The important thing is to trust your intuition, try to finish the exercises at the end of the chapters and keep a record of your progress in the "Diary" section. That way you can evaluate your progress once you finish the book.

Notice!

This book should be used as what it is meant to be: an instrument for bringing light and peace into the life of whoever reads it. Each line and exercise were inspired by divine love, seeking to bring all who read it into harmony with the universe and discover or remember their purpose on Earth. I'm not a therapist. If you think you have a serious problem, please see your doctor first.

Letter to the Reader

I began writing in the second grade of primary school, when my teachers noticed I had a special talent for storytelling. They gave me important positions, such as literature judge, despite my young age. This filled me with enthusiasm. My teachers encouraged me to develop my writing skills. I can safely say that that it is thanks to my primary school teachers that I'm a writer. Since then, I've written stories, fables, plays, poetry, and so on. Writing was always part of my life, but there was something else. Since I was a little girl, I noticed that I perceived the world differently, and I know I'm not the only one. I describe it as if I was born without that layer that covers or protects us from our environment. Many times, and of their own free will, there are people who decide not to perceive, not to know, not to connect with nature for fear of being hurt. I was born fragile and I'm not ashamed to admit it. I don't have that shell that covers most people, but it is that fragility that has paradoxically driven me to develop my heart and become the strong woman you know today. It was my sensitivity that forced me over time to study, to discipline myself and finally to be an instrument of inspiration for others.

My life hasn't been easy, I've gone through many bitter experiences which have forged a strong character within me. My childhood was very beautiful, despite not having my father by my side. I was a happy child thanks to my mother and my grandparents who always spoiled me a lot. I don't have very good memories of my adolescence, however, as it was at that time that I encountered internal conflicts because I didn't understand why I was somehow different from others. I remember that most of the time I spent outside in my backyard crying, admiring the stars and looking for an answer as to why I perceived things differently or why I was interested in subjects that others ignored.

Today I can say with both conviction and joy that I'm a happy woman. I live each day of my life intensely with an incredible happiness and inner peace that I would like to share with everyone. I've learned to balance my life and have managed to develop a technique for living in peace. I don't consider myself a spiritual teacher. Yet people have rewarded me with the honor of seeing in me a source of peace and inspiration, and it is my loyalty to people that keeps me from stopping my writing.

"What I Heard from a Star" is a book that is practical and easy to read, written with the intention of becoming a diary where you write down pieces of light from your soul.

You'll notice that in all the exercises I talk about "us" because we're together in this business of learning, being happy and trying to live in peace. I hope that by reading this book you'll feel the emotion and excitement that I felt when I wrote it.

Chapter 1: Clean-up Time

"I enlighten with thought those who allow me to caress their souls with my words. I balance all evil in my heart by cleansing it with love, thus learning to be an alchemist. Finally, I take the reins of my destiny."

Our lives are surrounded by energy, we ourselves are energy. We worry about cleaning our house and our cars, but we forget to clean our inner being. In our daily lives, we reflect what we have within us. Oftentimes in our homes we reflect how we feel on the inside. I know homeowners who are extremely attached to their memories, and their houses are overloaded with unnecessary objects. When people try to fill themselves with material things it's because they feel empty and they're trying to fill that space. Sadly, that void cannot be filled by material things.

You may wonder: "Laura, how do we clean our energy?" There are different techniques for cleaning our energy, and the results vary from person to person. After several years of practicing a variety of techniques, herbal baths and incense in the house, which in the end are limited to cleaning the aura, I've arrived at the conclusion that we should start by cleaning our minds. The mind is the source of all the problems and suffering that afflict us. We must stop negative thoughts before they lead to emotions which will end up making our bodies sick. If we try as much as possible to harbor positive thoughts, we'll notice that we're cultivating a bright future in our lives. Positive thinking is like planting a tree that will bear abundant fruit later on. When we keep our minds occupied with positive thoughts, we're more likely to have a spirit that is clear and serene. That way we can discern new paths that we magically see opening up before us. Suddenly we begin to see opportunities and doors we hadn't noticed before when we were confused and our minds were clouded, focused on our fears and doubts. We didn't even know those doors existed.

I propose that, from now on, we pay more attention to our thoughts, and that we do this impartially. Let's listen to them without feeling like we're judges, just as a mother would listen to her child. We'll notice that our fears often make us think a lot of things that don't make sense. If we listen to them attentively and with compassion, we'll even be more understanding of ourselves. We're letting our minds be saturated with unnecessary questions when deep down, when we're truly still and at peace, we know that everything will be all right. So then, why do we feed our fears? Let's begin by discerning each time a negative thought is about to be born and mentally say a word that we relate to pleasant things. Mine is "LOVE". By saying it mentally we nip any negative thought in the bud. This way we don't give it a chance to become an emotion that will be reflected in our mood later on and could even damage our health. We have the authority to strip negative thoughts of their power. At first that's all they are—thoughts that reflect our fears, and which are often ill-founded. The good news is that if we don't feed them, they will eventually disappear, and if we put positive thoughts in their place, we'll be transmuting that fear into joy. I'll talk in more detail later on about how to transmute the negative into positive.

To keep your heart clean, you must not only be careful about what you think, you must also watch what you say. We must try as much as possible to refrain from speaking ill of others. We must eradicate the bad habit of judging and criticizing from our hearts, and instead accept and understand that people are the result of their background, experiences and education. I know this part is difficult to implement. All of us at some point have complained about the postman, the cashier, people who have served us reluctantly at times, but we haven't stopped to think about what might be happening to that person. Even more, we haven't stopped to think that by complaining, the feeling that we're talking badly about others only affects us.

The truth is, we're all different. We're only responsible for our actions. We cannot, and must not, control or evaluate the actions of others. Sadly, we've been brought up in a society that constantly teaches us about criticism and competition. The immediate effect of every advertisement is to criticize ourselves and look for an immediate "solution" by buying a product we don't need to solve a problem we don't have. The reality we're offered is not the same as the one we live in; only a few understand this great truth. We don't need to look like they tell us to look in the magazines, our only obligation is to follow the voice of our soul. However, all of us at some point have criticized our physical appearance, lifestyle and so on for not being an exact copy of what the media sells us. The act of criticizing either our environment or ourselves places a heavy burden on us that is totally unnecessary in our lives. Many of us do it without realizing it, and the damage we do to ourselves accumulates daily. Whenever you feel like judging, speaking ill of someone or criticizing yourself, stop and bless your good qualities or those of that person. Everyone, without exception, has some good quality. In this way we'll be performing an exercise that nips all criticism in the bud and thus frees and cleanses us of the burden. Finally, the intelligent reason why we shouldn't criticize others is because everything we do to others, we're doing to ourselves. When you understand that principle, you'll realize that that's why when you do good you feel at peace. My intention is for you to remember your divinity. As you make peace with your spirit, you'll see how you begin to flourish. If you want to lose weight, you'll lose it because your body will tell you what to eat and what not to eat. The same goes for your heart. Your spirit will guide you in which steps to take in this spiritual adventure. You won't need to compare yourself to anyone else then; your only goal every day will be to become the best version of yourself.

However, in order to embark on the path to inner peace and complete happiness, we must cleanse our minds and hearts. We have the good will and the desire to persevere. Otherwise, we wouldn't be here keeping each other company. If we follow these practical exercises that I'll be showing you with conviction and sincerity, I guarantee a real change in your life. As you read this book, you'll remember your true essence, and it's my intention that you leave in the diary section all the feelings, bad habits or things from the past that haven't let you be happy and move forward until now.

When the mind and heart are clean, they are light, no longer dwelling on the past, no longer entertaining criticism or negative thoughts; instead they vibrate in love and peace, letting us shine as human beings. That's when life smiles at us differently. The grass is greener, the sunshine is brighter. Life begins to flourish when the heart is light, and the mind is clear as spring water.

Practical exercise

Everything that happens around us is a distraction, an illusion of what we really are. That is why meditation is so important, since it brings us closer to what we truly are, a divine essence alien to all death and error. We're an extension of divine love. Each day is a blank page, and we'll decide to fill it with either positive or negative thoughts. It's actually our responsibility, since we're the ones in control. Let's start by talking about meditation. How many people don't meditate because they think they have to wear exotic clothes, light incense and be part of the "new age?" If I may tell you, we have all meditated at some time. What do you like to do the most? Some will respond with listening to music or going to the movies, because thoughts dissipate at that time and it's like a mini mental vacation. Meditation is something like that. I'll try to explain it simply. Start with fifteen minutes, either lying down or sitting down, preferably using a little blanket. I want you to feel at ease. We're starting from scratch here, okay? Now choose some quiet music to accompany you on your journey. Music plays an important role in my meditations, as I consider it a portal that allows me to travel. Once you sit or lie down, listening to your favorite melody, preferably without lyrics, so it doesn't interfere with your subconscious, begin by paying attention to your breathing. As simple as that, you begin to be aware of your own breathing. You'll notice that it starts off a little fast and in a matter of minutes it calms down until you're super serene. There, I want you to watch as your ego disappears. You are not your name, your marital status, your thoughts or your problems. There you are. I want you to imagine a big board on which are written all the derogatory words that you ever said to yourself or someone else. I want you to take an eraser and start erasing them one by one. In their place, write nice things like healthy, smart, cheerful and so on, until you're satisfied. Then sign it and say goodbye to your sacred space. We'll come back later. Again, I want you to be aware of your breathing and count to yourself, 3, 2, 1 and open your eyes. You'll notice that you're in a very good mood. Congratulations! You've completed the first practical exercise in the book. Don't forget to read the tips and share your thoughts. It will be interesting to read how your thoughts have changed in a few months and at that time add your findings. Don't forget to share them with me. I'd like to be part of it.

Tips

- Be careful with our words as well as our thoughts, because from now on you'll be a completely new person.

- Practice silence and cultivate meditation as a means of learning by deciphering internal codes that reside in our spirit.

- Valuing words by making good use of them, reducing noise, creating music with our presence.

- This last one is one of my favorite tips, and I do it all the time. I call it "Love messages from my higher self." Leave love messages on your bedroom mirror, in the bathroom and in the kitchen. Say nice things, like "You can do anything," "You look prettier when you smile," "Expect good news." Reading these notes throughout the day generates anticipation and this emotion, when it's positive, generates encouragement. You'll notice that every time you read the notes it'll be like the first time, until you begin to notice that they're coming true.

I remember one time that I had left a note, "moments of love," in the corner of the mirror in my bathroom next to a small drawing of the Eiffel Tower. I didn't think much about it at the time, then a few months later I ended up visiting Paris for my birthday. It was during a romantic moment with my husband on that trip that I remembered my "moments of love" note.

We program our future every day. I hope these tips will bring you many smiles and times of love together with your loved ones.

Diary

What's the first word you'd use to describe yourself to someone who can't see you?

____

What did you feel when you erased the negative words on the board during the meditation?

____

____

____

____

____

____

____

Did you see anything else during the meditation? Write down all your doubts and fears. The idea is that as you practice and remember your essence, the fears and doubts will diminish, and a great love for your essence and an immense peace that envelops your heart will grow in their place. This is your sacred space. Here you can write and erase, grow and move forward.

____

____

____

____

____

____

____

____

____

____

____

____

Chapter 2: Establishing a Relationship with Nature

"May the wildflowers perfume your life and the light illumine your path. May nothing be so serious or so bad that it overshadows your spirit."

This is undoubtedly my favorite part of the book, as I've had a beautiful connection with nature since I was a child, and this has allowed me to learn a lot from it. I feel very sorry for us humans when we're wrapped in technology from head to toe and forget that we're walking trees. I could make a really long list of the experiences with nature that I've had throughout my life, which have been profound lessons for me, but my purpose in writing this book, in addition to inspiring in all of us an awakening of consciousness that brings us closer to our divinity, is to make our path to happiness practical, so I will limit myself to telling you about the last experience I had with nature.

A few years ago, I bought a little "money tree" plant and even brought it with me when I moved from New Jersey to Florida. I was a little worried that it would be affected by the climate change, but it survived. During these years I've seen it shed its leaves and grow many times, but this last year it didn't grow. I was sad. I decided to move it, and something wonderful happened. It grew and continues to grow as never before. So, I thought that all it needed to grow again was a change of place. But then I noticed something amazing. Another plant I had that was the same age—a bamboo—began to grow a new little branch. My happiness and amazement doubled. But the bamboo had not been moved, so the question occurred to me: did it grow because I moved it, or because my intention and energy suddenly changed?

I've had these plants for many years and I've never seen them so beautiful. And I finally understood that they're an extension of me. I thought that because they were so old and small in nature, it wasn't necessary for them to grow so much, but when the desire was born in me to see them grow, that positive change not only affected the money tree in a favorable way, but it affected all my little plants. There was a "miracle" effect since I had had these plants for many years and their size had always remained almost the same. This was the first time I'd ever seen them grow leafy.

So then, what lesson did nature teach me? It's worth getting rid of all the old leaves to grow new ones, it's worth it to start. Being born again is worth it. We're guided so often by what is logical, but love and nature teach us that there's another much greater force that is capable of proving to us that miracles do exist. Seeing both plants grow together at the same time really made me think that if I focus my attention with hope on a certain situation in my life, it will blossom.

How many times have we told ourselves, "It's too late for this," or "It's no use anymore," and we lose hope and take away the energy that fueled that dream? I'm telling you, don't do it. Whatever makes you sigh is worthy of your loving energy so that it will grow and flourish with you.

Don't waste any more time. Connect with nature. I bet you there are a lot of profound messages of love waiting for you. Flow with nature.

I'm going to share some practical exercises now so that, if you don't have that connection with nature yet, or if maybe you've lost it, you can connect with it. If you work in an office or live in a city, I'll give you some tips so you can have little bits of Mother Earth at your fingertips, with the aim of feeding and purifying your soul day by day. Don't forget to write down your experiences in the diary section as you put these exercises into practice. Let your soul speak freely and write down what you feel comes to you as a great answer. Remember that the intention of this book is to remind you of your divine essence. Messages will come, and I'm as excited as you are to discover all these treasures. For me, the spiritual path is a great adventure, and as the years have passed, I feel more comfortable being myself. So, believe me, when you are yourself, magical things begin to happen to you, and it even seems like the world has just been waiting for this great moment.

<u>Practical exercise</u>

I want to clarify what your intention should be in establishing a connection with nature. First, it is to purify you. Nature vibrates in such a highly pure way that the mere contact with a tree cleanses our aura immediately and makes us feel better. On days when you feel down, don't hesitate to put everything to one side and take a short walk. It only takes 15 minutes to be aware of your breathing and to admire your surroundings, each cloud in the sky, the grass, the trees and the little birds you'll see along the way. You'll notice that once you're in harmony with your spirit, you'll start reading what's going on around you. You'll see that the animals cross your path in numbers, and you'll see that that has to do with a question you'd been asking yourself. This would be the second intention, to connect with nature to send you important messages and lessons.

At one time in my life, I was not entirely happy in love. I was completely unhappy, and something very nice happened during one of my walks in the afternoon. Butterflies began to follow me in pairs; they followed me for a long time so I couldn't ignore them. That's how I noticed their beautiful relationship; one butterfly would fly away and the other would catch up with it, but they would always end up together. I understood the message and I began to cry from the emotion. Sometimes it's like that in life: we go on ahead and think we're alone, but the other person will catch up with us if they love us or vice versa. At that time, I felt in my heart that everything was going to be okay, and it was. Months later I was celebrating the pregnancy of my third child, Sebastian. Children are the purest representation of love on Earth.

Now that you know what the two intentions are when connecting with nature—purification and wisdom—I will share another of my favorite exercises with you, because when it comes to connecting with nature, the list of reasons to approach it is infinite, and the most important thing is to establish or re-establish the connection. As you do, you'll notice that you start being charged with positive energy. People who know me know I'm a mermaid with feet, so it's no surprise that one of my favorite exercises is to dip my feet in the ocean. This gesture purifies our soul almost immediately, symbolizing a cleansing and a new awakening.

Another very good one is to sit in front of the sun and let its light illuminate us and clean our thoughts. This exercise never fails me, I do it almost every afternoon, and I can literally feel its light recharge me with good energy. In the evenings if you can, spend some time to admire the stars. Shamelessly talk to the trees, touch them, hug them, connect with them. Give nature a chance to surprise you!

The relationship that each of us develops with nature is personal and intimate. Over time you'll be able to read the messages she sends you, sometimes in the form of birds flying over your head telling you that there is a message for you, other times in heart-shaped clouds telling you not to forget that love is everywhere. It's never too late to become friends with Mother Earth, to accept that she is sacred, to respect her and to love her.

<u>Tips</u>

- If you live in a city where access to nature or a park is limited, or you live in a place where the climate prevents you from going out for walks, this first piece of advice is for you. Try to find a small house plant like the one I mentioned at the beginning. Bamboo is an excellent choice. Look for a plant that you have a connection with and can have nearby. Maybe you can put it on your desk to remind you that even though you're in a building for a few hours, you're part of a big leafy family of beings that vibrate in love. It'll help you remember the vast expanse of the countryside and will put a smile on your face for sure.
- Get little semi-precious stones and keep them nearby. I usually put some in my plants and I think their

presence has benefited them as much as it has benefited me. My favorite semi-precious stones and their properties are

- o Rose Quartz: self-esteem and inner beauty
- o Sodalite: serenity and calm
- o Lapis Lazuli: communication and wisdom
- o Citrine: energy
- o Aventurine: luck and money
- o Tiger's Eye: strength and protection
- o Amethyst: peace of mind and protection
- o Moonstone: Regulates the menstrual cycle and communication between couples
- o White Opal: attracts true love and magical situations

I recommend having a rose quartz near your bedside table, your makeup or wallet so you always remember that first of all, you are the great love of your life and you must love, pamper, respect and give yourself all the care you deserve. I hope you have time to play with these stones and make them part of your life. They're a representation of the greatness and strength of nature.

- When you want to get together with friends, why not,

instead of meeting in a bar or restaurant surrounded by noise and distractions, opt for a walk in a park or at the shore of a lake? It is common that small animals such as birds, squirrels and even insects will cross our path on these walks. Don't take this as mere causality. Take note of their shape, their colors and stop to read what the universe is trying to tell you. Give your friends the greatest gift—your presence and your attention. Put your cell phone away! You'll observe that now you'll see more detail in people's eyes, you'll be more present than ever, you'll no longer feel that time is an executioner and slips through your fingers. You'll become the captain of the ship of your life and enjoy every minute of it.

The idea with these tips is to be present in every moment, enjoy the silence, and even if you're alone to notice that you never were. Now there are the stars, the owls and the clouds to keep you company. You'll feel that presence with a profound love and then you'll understand that you've always been connected to nature.

<u>**Diary**</u>

If you could choose a heavenly place in the world to enjoy a dream vacation, what would it be? Write down exactly where, how and who you'd like to be with. Describe every laugh, every activity you'd do and how much you'd enjoy it.

____

____

____

____

____

____

____

____

____

____

____

____

Now, when you're sad for whatever reason, I want you to come back to this page and read the dream of that vacation. The intention will be to program your mind to wish for the best in your life and not give space for the sadness to start programming an unpleasant future in your head.

You'll notice that step by step, you'll begin to make the change more easily and there will come a time when you won't need to read it because this desire will already be programmed into your subconscious. It won't be long before the universe will put all the pieces together and this great dream, however distant and impossible it may seem, will come true.

I'll leave an extra page for you to write down all the messages that nature sends you. Remember that at the beginning you won't notice them; at the beginning we're a little blind, but we gradually become aware that we must be present in every one of our activities. This means that if we're with a friend, we must be with the friend without thinking about what we're going to do tomorrow or checking our cell phone every five minutes. This act of being present makes us begin to appreciate every detail, and that's when the messages begin to rain down, not because they've just arrived, but because you've finally decided to let yourself see them.

Chapter 3: Recognizing our Senses

"The warmth of the sun slowly caresses us; the taste of that kiss remains on our lips even though the person has gone. That is the beautiful connection of our senses and reality. To recognize our senses is to awaken the memory of the soul."

The memory of the soul is achieved once we awaken each of our senses, once we stop to observe, caress, listen, speak and perceive. When we stop to live life that way, more attentive to its myriad details, we'll awaken to life in its fullness, rich in experiences, sensations and emotions. This life is our adventure and we have to pull out all the stops to really live it. To disconnect from our surroundings is to connect with our spirit, to open the gates of heaven and receive its light on our heads. It's the energy that comes from freeing ourselves from everything that ties us down and holds us back so that we can let our spirits fly. I've read this described in a variety of ways in a number of books, saying we should enjoy the now. This is my explanation. This is how I conjugate it with my signature romantic and dreamy air, so you understand that we must exude love from every pore. Recognizing and awakening our senses helps us be present in the here and now. Almost all of us live in a hurry because of what's going to happen later on, and we don't stop to live in the now. Others of us live tormented by the past and we don't let ourselves be happy in the now. The "now" is the time we all forget about and yet it's what we all take for granted. It's in this now that you're reading me, in this now that I'm writing to you. In this now you have the opportunity to drink a glass of water and feel how it caresses and revitalizes every organ in your body. It's in this now that you should be hugging the one you love and not waiting for tomorrow. Tomorrow is not now.

It's important that you make peace with the present. Today we live in a collective reality that rushes us to celebrate a date that hasn't arrived on the calendar yet; the busiest person is acclaimed, but we rarely stop to ask, is he or she happy? I want you to imagine that life is a race. Suddenly you stop and say, "I'm not running anymore." That's when you'll really be able to smell the roses and smile. Do you know what will happen? Life will adjust itself to your pace. It's not that it wasn't going fast in the first place, it's just that that's the way we've been taught to live. Eat fast or you'll miss the bus, finish up soon so you can graduate. Don't worry, the weekend's coming and when it does, when these moments pass, we hope there will be more to come. And so, we never enjoy the present.

I love my children so much because, among other things, in their chaos as children, they force me to live in the present. My youngest son doesn't care if I'm late. The most important thing for him is that I look out the window and see the monkey in the tree, even if that little monkey is imaginary. I end up laughing and this leads to my attention being drawn to his face. There I realize how he has grown and that his eyes turn honey colored in the sun. All of a sudden, he hugs me and says, "I love you." This is all I care about in life. So, I can't rush, I must not rush. No matter where people go in such a rush, I will always stop and look into the eyes of my loved ones to tell them how much I love them. That's my proposal, that we organize our lives a little so we can let ourselves "waste time" with those we love and need. Organize a real future without neglecting what's most important—ourselves.

In this chapter I propose that we establish a different perspective when thinking about our senses, remembering that they let us be present in every act of our life and thus enjoy each one to the full. Let's talk about taste. When it comes to eating, you have to learn to taste your food, not eat in a hurry, no matter how much work or studying you have to do, nothing will ever be more important than your health. You should plan time to eat and enjoy your meals.

As for hearing, may the music you listen to feed your spirit, with melodies and lyrics that affect your subconscious positively. It's time to be more discriminating when it comes to feeding our bodies, and I don't just mean food. Music is food too! You should make sure it does you good and helps you grow instead of making you moody, sad, or unconsciously repeating things like "I'm a mess."

When you talk with your loved ones, listen to them, seriously this time, noticing the emphasis they place on certain words and the special way they pronounce them. It'll help you admire them more profoundly and better understand what they're trying to tell you.

Let's talk about touch now. I confess that I hate to fold clothes! It feels almost like a medieval punishment, but when I start to feel the texture of my clothes, I feel a great love for every sweater that keeps me warm, for the softness of the fabric that caresses and covers me. Right there at that precise time everything changes, I'm present in love and gratitude, and an activity that would be tedious for me becomes an act of unconditional love instead.

Smell is essential. Have you noticed that every house has a particular smell, and when you perceive it you remember all the moments you lived there? Imagine if you let yourself be surrounded by the smells that please you the most and that lift up your spirit. One of my favorite soaps is lavender, so on busy days, when I may not have time to linger in the tub for a long time, the scent of lavender relaxes me and helps me dedicate that bath time to renewing my energy through the water. In the same way, the smell of bread reminds many of us of our grandparents. For me, the smell of freshly baked chocolate cookies, and basically, a host of other smells bring back unforgettable memories that put a smile on my face. Right now, at this very moment, we're creating memories. Try to surround yourself with aromas that lift your spirits and make you feel happy. My favorite aromas are floral, and it's common for me to anoint myself with oils as the day unfolds. I feel they help sharpen my senses. I want you to be aware of the importance of smell in helping us be present in our common and mundane activities in such a way that we turn them into sacred acts that later on will become memories that we'll treasure forever.

Sight is the sense that many of us take for granted, and we go through life without appreciating all its colors. The truth is that I'm not very fond of people who observe people closely and pay too much attention to what they wear, but I would be lying if I told you I don't notice people's faces. It's important for me to read every gesture, and in a matter of minutes I'll know if you're sad, happy, angry, or if you're hiding something from me. I can't help it, since I was little, "that's the way I was." Over time I've tried to use this gift to help the person change his or her mood if I notice they're sad or troubled. Someone who needs a hug couldn't cross my path without my stopping to give them my full attention. That's what sight is all about—seeing—but seeing more than just clothes, fashions, and even what people often want us to believe is their reality and what they post on their social networks. My invitation is to see beyond, to see their eyes when they're in front of you, to see their aura, how your heart reacts when you have them close to you. It has happened to me that I know people who describe themselves as "bad" who bring out an incredible tenderness in me when I have them around, and also the opposite, feeling repulsion when I'm around people who call themselves "good."

To be awake to the senses is to fully appreciate who we are and thus easily realize who the people who approach us truly are. Our senses bring us closer to ourselves, to our memories of the soul, and at the same time they act as a defense mechanism that tells us who to look out for or stay away from in our life.

Follow the signs, listen to your soul, don't go for the logical or real, go for what your internal compass tells you. It knows more than anyone, it's so wise, and you can connect to this great master through your senses.

<u>Practical exercise</u>

Begin on your own by listening to your steps as you walk, listening in detail to all the sounds around you. You'll end up concentrating on your own body sounds such as your heartbeat. This exercise will not only help you awaken your senses, it will connect you directly with your being, awakening in you a love, affection and respect for your person that will be reflected in your surroundings later on. Then, observe and admire your actions in detail when you're in the company of others. Give yourself the luxury of admiring your life in slow motion, don't hurry when people are rushing you; that's when you must slow down. After performing this exercise for a while, you'll notice that you're more beautiful than you thought you were, that your neighbor isn't all that unpleasant, that days aren't over so quickly, that Mondays aren't so ugly. In short, you'll begin to live as you should—happily and in harmony.

A practical way to incorporate this into your daily life is to leave little notes as I mentioned at the beginning of the book, in this case telling yourself to "stop for a while and smile." Believe me, no matter how busy you are or what a bad mood you're in that day, you'll stop and smile, thus creating the intention to change the course of the day, and a day that might have been heading for a dreary end will wind up being happy and hopeful.

Tips

- Surround yourself with foods with vibrant colors and

aromas that lift your spirits.

- Give yourself a big hug and tell yourself: "I'm really proud of you," then take your hands and say: "I'll always be there for you." As small and insignificant as these acts may seem, they strengthen the relationship you have with yourself. No one is more important than you. When you understand that from an understanding outside the ego, you'll know that you need to love yourself this strongly in order to love everyone around you, that you need to be there for yourself. Be strong, and then you can be strong and determined for those who need you.

- Perfume yourself with a smell that is natural and pleasant. My favorites are coconut and roses. When I apply coconut to my hair it reminds me of the beach, and roses make me feel loved.

- Remember to fill every moment with decorations, food and smells that make you happy. This is your paradise.

<u>**Diary**</u>

Describe one of your happiest memories. What were you wearing? What did it smell like? Was it day or night? Etc.

Make a list of your favorite foods, colors and smells. Are you surrounded by these ingredients in your life? If not, make a note of what you would like to incorporate that would bring you joy. In my case, I'd like to have a hammock and make myself coconut shakes. I'm sure you also have desires to fulfill, and that's the beauty of consciously enjoying your life.

____

____

____

____

____

____

____

____

____

____

____

____

Chapter 4: Feed Your Soul

"The beauty of life, the timelessness of the memory of a kiss, the purest essence of life captured in a verse… That is writing, that feeds my soul."

My soul feeds on landscapes, poetry and Celtic music. What does your soul feed on? What does it ask for? What does it thirst for? Like the body, the soul needs nourishment, and we often make the mistake of expecting someone else to feed our soul. If we think about it, when we're hungry, we just look for food, it's our survival instinct. It should be the same with the desires of our soul. The soul feeds on things that are intangible but sublime. It feeds on music, on a landscape, on an expression of endearment. The collective soul is hungry for beauty, love and peace. We human beings worry about dressing our bodies and feeding our egos, but we leave the soul to one side and that's where great emptiness comes from, and hence depression. We must not wait for that kind of invitation to feed the soul; it's up to us to seek its nourishment. The fabulous news I have is that food for our soul is completely free and always abundant. To feed the soul we just need to learn to recognize our senses, what we talked about in the previous chapter, and thus perceive the world differently, situate ourselves in the present, the now. Little by little and effortlessly, stripped of prejudice, armed only with hope, we'll understand that to live in peace we must unlearn and disengage ourselves from any concept and idea that distances us from our origin. When we reach that point, we'll be ready to listen directly to our soul, without interference. It will reveal to us what it feeds on.

I know professionals with lots of money and successful careers, and yet they're depressed because they never took the time to do what their souls asked of them. It's as if they're waiting for someone to give them permission to do it. "I'm waiting for my kids to grow up and then I'll go sailing." "I'll wait till summer's over and then I'll call that girl I met at the beach." Again, we fall into the cycle of waiting for tomorrow and forgetting about now, of underestimating the soul's desires and longings in order to calm the "more important ones" according to the needs society has imposed on us. The truth is that if we neglect the soul it doesn't matter how much success, fame or money we have, everything will fall apart. I'm not talking about something tangible. There are many millionaires who feel miserable because they have nothing, only money. They have no values, no desires, no desire to smile from the soul because it died with no one to feed it.

I think the most important part here is defining what feeds your soul. In my case, since I love writing poetry, my great nourishment is inspiration. I'm usually inspired by melodies, my favorite being Yanni's piano music. I'm inspired by people's humility and the peace of nature, which moves me and makes me fall in love.

Try to listen to your soul and be honest with yourself. What really makes you happy? What moves you? What are you passionate about? Your answers to these questions are what feeds your soul. Sometimes it's something as simple as a sunset. I've noticed that my soul loves solitude and feeds on the peace that comes with silence. That doesn't mean I don't love the company of my loved ones, but I've learned to listen to my soul and give it what it asks for. In those moments of solitude and silence I not only feed my soul, I discover wonderful things about myself and return to share them with a renewed and strengthened spirit. To be truly healthy, feeding our soul is as important as feeding our body.

Practical exercise

Start by observing your reaction to things, situations, words, landscapes. Have you ever marveled at a shooting star? Sighed at a sunset? That's your food! Continually seek out those experiences that amaze you, make you sigh or fall in love. For me personally I have a fascination for birds. I like to see them fly, I like to see their colors and the way they interact. I enjoy that, and I marvel at it, no matter how many times it happens. Every surprise, every sigh, every smile is a glass of water for the soul. Give it a drink every day and then let yourself be happy every day.

Set aside at least five minutes of your lunch or break, so that when you finish eating you have that time to do whatever you love. As short as that sounds, if you do it all week, it will be thirty-five minutes that you will have dedicated to what you love. The important thing is that it is an activity that feeds your spirit and then leaves you with a feeling of renewal.

In my case, I try to read at least one paragraph of my favorite books, listen to one of my favorite songs, sing and definitely dance. Who doesn't have 5 minutes a day to do what they love?

<u>Tips</u>

- When the weekend comes, leave your obligations until last. Yes, you read me right. First make sure you feel good. After you have checked with your inner self—"Am I okay? What do I need?"—and dedicated at least 5 minutes to an activity that brings you emotional peace and joy, you can go on to whatever you had planned for your day, weekend or vacation.

- The problem with the modern world is that we barely get up, or whenever we have some extra time, we spend it on anything but ourselves, and no, uploading photos to social networks does not count as time for us. I want you to pay attention to yourself, listen to yourself, pamper yourself, and when you have spent a few minutes doing that, carry on. It won't take you forever, it'll only be a few minutes, but that intention to change our perspective from "first everything else and then me", to "I'll always go first and then everything else", that is what will enable you to always be alert, happy and animated with your life project.

Diary

When was the first time you felt love for yourself? When was the first time you felt proud of your achievements? If your answer is "never," I want you to run to the first mirror you find, congratulate yourself and say: I love you, I'm proud of you! Share here your emotions, experiences and so on. It will be exciting to read them later, and it will definitely be a great memory during this great adventure to be able to come back and read the wonderful things you were discovering, remembering and living.

____

____

____

____

____

____

____

Chapter 5: Play and Smile

"Blessed are the children who remind us that to play is to live."

Let's try to surround ourselves with positive energy, such as the love of people who appreciate us, because this is our story, it's our life and we have to live it with joy. There's always someone in the family or social circle who's the life of the party, and many times they'll get a smile out of us, even in the midst of tears. These people are angels, they're happy, noble souls. An adult who smiles at simple situations in life is a child who has survived the passage of time. Blessed are the people who can make us smile.
We're almost always tuned in to problems to the point that we look like our problems—serious and boring. Taking time to play and smile is taking time to meditate. Meditating is not as complicated as it seems. Meditation is simply a cleansing of our thoughts, and I can't think of a more effective technique than having a good time with friends.

It's so healthy to learn to fall in love with the essence of people, to breathe the peace of the universe, to love everyone as ourselves. For today, try not to get angry, try to be fair. At least try because we understand that we're human. There's already something divine in just trying to do that. Smile and greet others even if they're not nice. You'll be surprised by the barriers that a smile brings down. Enjoy every moment. Dream that everything is possible. In other words, Live with hope! If you let yourself play and smile as a daily practice in your life, you'll notice that when you have magic in your eyes, the world is transformed, words are alive, and love becomes a pair of wings.

During my childhood in Ecuador, I was the kind of girl who sat out recess because she didn't want to get dirty. I watched everything from my seat and almost everyone thought that since I was the best student I was probably very serious, but when you got to know me you realized that I was very funny, I liked to do imitations and make up characters. The truth is that I was the opposite of what I looked like, but only people who dared to cross the barrier of my apparent seriousness got to know me. Now that I analyze myself as an adult, maybe that was my protection tactic. Now, imagine how many people you've missed meeting because you thought they were so serious. I'm very happy for those people who dared to approach me and became my friends.

So, I invite you to smile at everyone. I would say that it's even more important to smile at those who look the most serious because they might need to meet that someone who invites them to be themselves without fear. I'm sure you'll be pleasantly surprised like my little friends in elementary school.

By the time I was in high school, I had become a little more assertive, and I think that in my youth and up to the present day, I've been very much myself. I would laugh out loud so much that when I moved to the United States, I was reprimanded for laughing at everything. They made me believe that something was wrong with me. Thank God I never listened to them, I never changed! I've always kept my sense of humor, even in my worst circumstances, and this made them more bearable. Being a bit of a clown is part of me and you don't know how much I love that about me!

Recently I had to travel to my native Ecuador urgently, because of my grandmother. She's quite elderly and all of a sudden, she became very ill and had to be hospitalized.

The truth is that I was very sad. I stayed in a hotel where everyone who worked there, without knowing my situation, was extremely kind and good to me. The day I was the saddest because my grandmother wasn't getting any better, I ordered my lunch from the room. When I finished I called for the dishes to be picked up, and after the hotel employee took the tray, I realized that I had forgotten one of the dishes on the table, so I called again to ask them to please send someone to pick it up. Not five minutes later, the same hotel employee arrived, greeted me and said, "That's a good girl. Now, will you?" Then he burst out laughing. What pure laughter! I looked into his eyes and I swear I saw the purity I had in school. I saw a good man, without prejudice. I saw that complicity between humans in his eyes, something that's been lost over the years and for which I love my Ecuador so much, where people still have that purity, where they still laugh with their whole soul and you can have friends for life. That hotel employee may never know that he inspired me to write these lines. He made me smile despite my pain, and that is the miracle that playing and smiling brings about in life. No matter the age, no matter the situation, laughing is healthy, playing brings us together.

Practical exercise

When you get up and brush your teeth, look in the mirror and smile. That way you decree that your day will be a pleasant one. I've often heard that about smiling, and I think it's nice and practical, but I'd throw in a couple of crazy expressions too, maybe stick out your tongue while you comb your hair. You'll see yourself having a couple of good laughs because you'll feel like a kid again. That's the idea—loosen up, get free, let yourself be playful and funny. As the day goes by, give yourself permission to be playful with those you trust, too. Crack jokes, dance in the elevator when it's empty, tell a joke even if you're the only one who laughs. Give yourself the luxury of a smile as a greeting in a shop. You'll spread love and kindness. It seems like a tiny act, but a good-humored person spreads that joy and those good vibes around the world. It's a small act, but it has a big and positive impact on your surroundings. Make an appointment with a friend or your significant other to play in the park, let yourself be a child for a day and live it up, buy yourself an ice cream of five different flavors, prance around, kick up your heels. Did you know you can still do that? Call your parents if you're lucky enough to have them alive and ask them to tell you the biggest prank you ever pulled as a kid. That'll wake up your inner child who's still there, just asleep. Pretend you can see the world with the same enthusiasm and happiness you had as a child and without shame let yourself smile.

<u>Tips</u>

- In the notes I've recommended that you leave for yourself, draw a couple of happy faces. On the days you don't feel quite right, put up more happy faces, write phrases like "I'm healthy and happy" or "I'm happy to be the way I am." Accepting ourselves brings the greatest of joys into our lives.

I guarantee that no matter what trials you face in life, you'll always have reasons to smile, and invite those you love to smile with you.

<u>Diary</u>

Think back to a day when you were rather pessimistic and serious. Change it. Write about what your day would have been like if you'd taken things less seriously and with more humor instead. Then read it. You'll be surprised how much you'll learn about yourself. Sometimes seriousness is the armor that we impose on our surroundings to keep people from hurting us, but that armor is what keeps us from enjoying life.

____

____

____

____

____

____

____

____

____

____

Chapter 6: Recognizing Our Strength

"The world needs good people who are not afraid to do good. The world needs heroes of love and goodwill."

When you need the strength to keep on keeping on, don't look outside, look inside. Let me tell you, it's not too late to dream. Believe in miracles, and miracles will believe in you. Let love expand from the inside of you to the outside. Love and dream, help and create. Do your little bit to make this world a better place to live. I remember once that a butterfly got into my house. I noticed it flying a little clumsily, so I carefully covered it with a napkin and then let it fly free in the garden. I stayed there looking at it for a while. It flew in front of me majestically, putting a smile on my face. Then I thought, this is how we feel when we're finally in the right place—we're free and happy. It's time to let ourselves go with the force that determines the right path for us. At the end of the day, you have to be who you are, no matter what everyone else is. Do good without expecting anything in return. If people act badly, that action remains in them and will bear the corresponding fruit throughout their lives. We must rescue the values that our ancestors instilled in us. The world needs good people who are not afraid to do good. The world needs heroes of love and goodwill.

Let's start listening to our inner voice, the one we so often despise and doubt. Let's cover our fears with courage because having the courage to be yourself means having the courage to give up everything that is not necessary for growth.

Start by recognizing, appreciating and listening to that inner voice. That's where your strength lies. What you feel in your bosom is your guide, your engine. Don't kill its desire to grow and become an idea, a life. Let that voice out, let it grow. We must lose the fear of daring to be happy, we must start to be more daring and enjoy our life. Throughout my life I've had to face situations which I thought were too difficult or too big for me, but I believe that I never faced them alone. In the darkest moment of our lives, when we go really deep down, something wonderful happens and we realize what we're made of. It's there that we connect with this divine source that feeds us, that gives us life and that keeps us on our feet. It's there that we emerge, keep on going and succeed, and then we feel stronger than ever.

I'm going to share a very personal experience with you but I think it's necessary for me to open up, so you can do the same here in the diary section and we can move forward in this beautiful adventure of life. As you know, in my childhood and adolescence I was very devoted to my beliefs, I had a tremendous faith which kept me happy and serene. At the age of 18 I left Ecuador to study in the United States. When I started my university studies, I took a philosophy class with a professor who was very convincing when talking about why we shouldn't believe in anything. It was a very unstable time for me, and I felt a little strange. I'd had my first romantic break-up and the disappointment was eating away at my soul. I was far from my country, family and friends and sought comfort in my studies. Sadly, these theories took away what I believed in and the change in me was devastating. I became a zombie and walked the streets dejectedly. I didn't understand what was going on around me. I was in pain and I felt helpless.

I didn't realize that my beliefs, God, the light, dreaming with my eyes open were the force that fed me and kept me alive, happy and optimistic. I put all that aside because now that I was in college I was "grown up" and could no longer believe in dreams, in things I couldn't prove, in fantasies that weren't based on logic. Then I realized I was wrong. I had to be very sad and lost to remember the way. There were days when I missed myself, missed my laughter, missed dreaming while looking at the stars. Where had I gone? One of those days when I was very sad as I went to sleep, I dreamed that I was in paradise, swimming next to a beautiful swan. Suddenly a voice said to me: "Paradise is on earth." I woke up with this huge doubt in my head: how could this be possible? I, who had questioned all my beliefs because of new theories, was now dreaming that paradise was on Earth. It made no sense. That day things started to change for me; it was like the universe was trying to get through to me through dreams. On another occasion, I had the same dream but this time I was told that I should write. I woke up a little confused and started keeping a journal of these dreams. During those months, I had more dreams, some of which came true. The most special of them all, when I was about to finish college, was one in which I was lost in a temple and a beautiful little girl no more than 4 years old was showing me the way out. I remember so clearly what she looked like—she had jet black curly hair and a contagious smile. She was wearing a white dress that went all the way down to her bare little feet. When I said goodbye, I asked her who she was, and she said she was my daughter. My daughter? I didn't even have a boyfriend! A year later, as life would have it, I had my firstborn—Danyella, who turned out to be as beautiful as she was in my dream. I have a lot of fun now telling her that story.

What I'm getting at is that the time I was weakest in my life was the time I became disassociated from my essence. My essence is uncommon, it has no logic for many, it speaks of the strength of hope and faith, of dreams that connect with heaven and other realities and sometimes predict the future, but all that magic is me. The moment I accepted myself without any doubts, without fear of being judged or criticized, that was the moment I discovered my strength. What's your strength? I invite you to discover it! If you're afraid to discover it because you feel lonely, take my hand, I'm here with you through this book. I bet you already know it. Your strength was born with you, it's the essence that makes you so unique and can lead you to make the most important dreams of your life come true.

Practical exercise

Find a quiet moment in the day when you can go to the place where you're the most comfortable and calm. In stillness try to listen to your inner voice with patience and love. That's how you'll find out what your essence is. Your essence is your strength. Let your soul guide you, follow the signs that the universe sends you, and launch yourself into living the greatest adventure of your life. Whether it's a dream, something that catches your attention on the radio, or a word from a friend, messages come from many different places. The important thing is to have the intention of discovering or rediscovering our essence, to wrap ourselves in this great force in order to reach our goals and be happy.

We're going to use this meditation to discover our essence. Like I said before, look for a comfortable place that you consider sacred, whether it's a chair or your bed. Get comfortable but try not to fall asleep. Start paying attention to your breath, I want you to start with three deep breaths and exhalations. When you inhale, imagine you're feeding on golden light, and when you exhale, you expel everything that's no good to you—your nervousness and doubts. Now I want you to close your eyes and imagine yourself going to a magical garden. Feel how nature surrounds you, you perceive the aroma of flowers, green grass on the soles of your feet, blue skies and large, leafy trees, blue, orange and yellow birds flying around you together with beautifully colored butterflies. Suddenly, in the distance, you see a hawk inviting you to follow it. It shows you a beautiful lake; you follow it and dive into the lake. The water is clear as crystal and you feel as if your soul is being cleansed. When you come out of the lake you find three chests. Try to open one, it doesn't matter which one. There you'll find a clue about your essence and strength.

You can do this exercise as many times as you want and yes, you can receive as many hints as you need. Imagination knows no limits.

I give you my personal example: being a writer, I feed on words and poetry. The place where my soul takes me is the sea, the beach is where my spirit is recharged, my strength is the water. Water is my essence, the source of my poetry.

When I'm weak, I look for words, I look for poetry and I almost always end up sitting on a beach, facing the sea, writing. When I go back home, I'm stronger than ever. Communing with our essence increases our strength. My wish is that you'll remember your essence and also remember that you've never been alone.

Tips

- Think about the characters in history that you admire the most for their strength and trajectory.
- Write down their names and keep them on hand for days when you need inspiration and motivation.
- You can also print their photos and remember the strength and tenacity they have or had to make their dreams come true.

The day will come when it will be your name and your own photo that will inspire you with strength and courage. You're braver, more powerful and more capable than you think.

<u>**Diary**</u>

When was the last time you had to be strong? I'd like you to write a letter to your child self, telling him/her that everything will be all right. You'll see how strong and capable you are. You'll also notice the infinite love that you feel for yourself. If you want to apologize for having been afraid, do it. It's also worth it to give big hugs and tell that child you'll always be there to comfort him/her. And the most important thing is to tell him/her not to worry, to keep playing, that everything will be fine.

____

____

____

____

____

____

____

____

Chapter 7: Multiplying Our Blessings

"I don't know if I'm an angel, but I'd like to be your angel, cover you with my wings from all evil and in an embrace fill you with peace."

Let's examine the concept of happiness. There is no happiness for a person who is selfish, much less for one who is arrogant. That's why they say that money doesn't buy happiness. If you have never fed a sick child, if you have never offered your hand to an old man crossing the street, I invite you to do it now! Let's gradually change the concept of happiness. Today may be the day your heart feels so light that you see the stars and finally smile. In the end, to receive love, one must feel love, breathe love, love, become love. To feel peace, you have to breathe peace, give peace, be a medium of peace. Our life reflects our feelings. What do you feel in your heart right now? We must focus our attention on what we have and not on what we lack. Magnify the sun that shines on us and not the shadow that pursues us. We'll always find reasons to cry, but if we want to, we can find infinite reasons to smile. They can strip us of everything material, the world can come crashing down, but if we're able to keep our good memories alive and our love intact in a clean heart, we can create a new world out of nothing.

It is very easy for me to notice people who are unhappy. They might be healthy or live in luxury, but they're incredibly unhappy. It seems that the more things they have, the emptier they feel. These are the people who have never stopped to perceive anything beyond their noses. When people focus on ways to help others they begin to be truly blessed and realize how blessed they are. Because that is everyone's mission: TO HELP. All our actions are like a boomerang that comes back to us sooner or later. The love you gave with all your soul—even if the person you gave it to hasn't known how to benefit from it—is energy that will return to you, even if in the form of a flower. When we discover that everything we give comes back, many times multiplied, we begin to feel much freer to give ourselves. We should no longer fear being disappointed, betrayed or disillusioned. We don't have to expect anything in return. The energy of love is never lost. Ideally, it will return as we wish, but who are we to determine how things should be? We must let the universe vibrate, while we tune in to it. Give hugs that come back in song. Give kisses that grow into poetry. To be an inspiration, to be a warm kiss on the lips of someone who dreams of you and never dreamed of seeing you so close. Life can really be wonderful when you stop waiting and let yourself be surprised.

Practical exercise

Try to act spontaneously, don't self-censor yourself. We all in some way have that natural need to help the neediest, but for lack of time or money we don't. We say, "well, that's why there are organizations that take care of that," or "there are people with more money," and we end up convincing ourselves not to do it. If we let ourselves act naturally, we'd be helping make this world a more beautiful place to live in. Giving without expecting to receive anything in return, if we all acted in this way innocence would be ignited and so much selfishness would be cleansed. We would definitely multiply our blessings and ultimately, we'd be happier!

Meditation to light the flame of blessings: look for a comfortable place that you consider sacred, whether it's a chair or your bed. Get comfortable but try not to fall asleep. Start paying attention to your breath, I want you to start with three deep breaths and exhalations. When you inhale, imagine you're feeding on golden light, see the word "thanks" in your mind, and when you exhale, expel everything that's no good to us, like a gray cloud that travels to the ends of the universe. There, far away from us, it will become something positive. Then I want you to imagine that you open a door and discover a room where you find all your most precious treasures, from your childhood up to the present. Suddenly you notice that there's a beautiful window facing the sea. You see how the sea in its swaying brings you gifts on the shore. From a distance you can see how they shine and that causes you emotion and joy.

I want you to keep that feeling throughout the day. Being receptive to gifts brings positive things. Imagine how nice it would be to wake up feeling like it's Christmas every day. What gift will life give me? You know you deserve the best, you know that, right? Let's keep that feeling of gratitude and surprise, it's worth it to feel excitement for living.

Tips

- Find a gift box and write down all your gifts inside, as you remember them, keep writing them down, more and more. When you're feeling a little down, open this box. How could someone with so many gifts and blessings be sad?
- Leave this little box where you can see it. Just seeing it, that alone generates a positive result in your state of mind.

Diary

Write down the months of the year and next to them write down what you would like to happen. Let's do an experiment. Don't ask for anything, in effect, just be grateful. For example, I'd like to go back to Paris. I would say, "I'm grateful that I have the opportunity to return to a place as magical as Paris." To be thankful for what has yet to be received or what hasn't happened is a great display of faith. Faith is the miracle ingredient that makes everything—absolutely everything—possible. Never doubt. Doubt is the kryptonite of every Superman.

____

____

____

____

____

____

____

____

____

____

____

____

____

____

Chapter 8: Transmute

"Enlighten with thought those who allow me to caress their souls with my words. Balance all evil in my heart by cleansing it with love, thus learning to be an alchemist. Finally, take the reins of my own destiny."

To live happily and healthily we must constantly cleanse our minds and spirits. Forget about the constant guilt and judgments coming from the rest of the world and ourselves. Begin to take responsibility for creating an environment of peace and love in our homes, offices and everywhere we visit, thus spreading love and peace throughout the world. We have been led to believe that we cannot change the world, and the truth is that we can. Together we can do anything we put our minds to. Everything is possible. The fights, the disagreements, the sorrows and the anguish are part of our development as human beings. Every experience in our life, good or bad, is necessary for our evolution. Forgiving and forgetting is not a sign of weakness as many people believe; it's an act of respect and courage for our own being. The only way to be reborn is to transform the soul, leaving behind all that is bad, cleansing the path of our life, thus opening the windows of our spirit to a life full of peace and happiness. It's important sometimes to try to disconnect from our surroundings in order to connect with our spirit. In this way we'll open the gates of heaven and receive its light on our heads. By establishing a direct contact with our being, we'll activate the universal love that dwells in all of us. That love is the energy that comes to free us from everything that ties us down and holds us back, that doesn't let us be happy.

In the process there will be moments of doubt, moments when we'll focus our attention on mundane things or simply be victims of a toxic environment and toxic people, which create an illusion of prison. We think that we don't have the power or freedom to take control of our life or of certain situations. The truth is that we all have the right to say no, to say that's enough and to wipe the slate clean. We're all entitled to a new awakening. Once this stage is over, you'll know that there's a light inside you that shines, and you'll know it because it'll be so strong and so incandescent that no one will be able to turn it off— nobody, not even you. Shallow people make fun of people who try to see life more profoundly, yet we're all part of the balance. We need people who doubt in order to believe. We need things that are not true for something to be true. That is why the best weapon to attack those who criticize us and try to harm us is to love them. Yes, love them. Then comes forgiveness and later absolute forgetfulness of everything that once hurt you.

Practical exercise

Look for a comfortable place that you consider sacred, whether it's in a chair or your bed. Get comfortable but try not to fall asleep. Start by paying attention to your breath, I want you to start with three deep breaths and exhalations. When you inhale, imagine you're feeding on a golden light that revitalizes all your organs, and when you exhale, say goodbye to all your fears, doubts and the stress that has built up during the day. Now I want you to close your eyes and imagine that your heart is a purple ball of fire and that everything that touches it is transformed into a beautiful dove that takes flight. Now imagine your heart coming to people who hurt you very much at some point. You see them transform into doves and now they fly away into the sky, leaving you with a sense of peace and freedom. What you've done right now is an exercise in transformation and forgiveness. What happens in a symbolic way in our imagination, happens in an emotional way in our senses, registering it in our mind and memories as something that actually happened. Welcome to the world of alchemy! Feel free to play with your imagination and cleanse your heart, as many times as necessary, in this violet flame. Violet energy is a highly positive energy, it can change, heal and transmute situations. Love is just as powerful when it comes to healing, that's why it's so important to love and to let yourself be loved but in an unconditional and universal way. That is the pure way children and animals love, the way we have forgotten but will remember together.

<u>Tips</u>

- Write a letter to that person who at some point in your life did you wrong, tell them everything you think, then take this letter and take it to a river, lake or the sea and let it go. If you don't have access to anywhere like that, put it in a drawer and visualize this person picking it up and reading it. After an hour, tear it in pieces and throw it away, imagining how, together with this letter, you let go of all the feelings of anger, sorrow or resentment.

- On days when you feel heavy in your soul because issues from the past are pursuing you, look for a piece of paper and write down how you feel— "sad", for example. Then cross it out and say goodbye by throwing it in the trash. In its place, write another note that says "happy" and leave it near a picture of you or under your pillow.

- We are what we think, and we think what we feel. So then, let's feel nice things, shall we?

<u>Diary</u>

Write exactly how you would like to be treated, exactly how you would like to be spoken to, what you would like to be told. Now I want you to start treating people this way. At first, you'll feel that they don't deserve it, or sometimes people won't understand why you're so nice (believe me, this happens all the time) but just do it. Remember at the beginning I told you that what you do for others you do for yourself? Soon you'll notice that people—even some who barely know you—start treating you the way you wanted so badly for them to treat you.

Chapter 9: Practicing Universal Love

"Immortal love, deep expression of our spirit, love that transcends time, seas, flesh and sex. Love that can heal the sickest, wake from the deepest sleep and make the most blind see."

It is easy to fall into the nets of false love that creates the illusion of belonging, when in reality no one owns anything, much less someone else. Love is free, love is freedom. Learn to see beyond things, learn to feel beyond sensations. There's a hidden world, one you're unaware of with your eyes open. Close your eyes and open your heart. I promise you that little by little you'll begin to see a different world. A clean heart projects universal love that shatters mental chains. Let's use our hands to work for peace and let our tears sprout seeds from which new hope will emerge. Nothing can harm or destroy you as long as you cover yourself with this love. You will never believe in spells, diseases or obstacles. Love will make you incredulous of anything that doesn't vibrate at its level. I've read many books, got a degree, but what I'm writing here is the result of my tears, which cleaned my soul and transformed me into an instrument of peace. I believe in you and I know you'll succeed in filling your heart with love. We're going to practice universal love together to make this world a better place to live in, for my children and yours, for generations to come.

Begin to understand that each person's every act is the result of their experiences, education and environment. That way you'll understand why some people act better than others. Compassion is the greatest gift of our time. You have noticed that more and more people are daring to live their truth, even though there are still crimes of racial hatred or homophobia. It's painful. Sometimes it seems that no matter how much we do to fight for our rights of equality and have the courage to express our soul, there will always be people who are deranged and bad. That should not change our perspective of change at all, nor should it soil our hearts. On the contrary, it should motivate us to continue being an earthly angel and to pass on this knowledge, this conviction of love to our family and friends, so that soon there will be more of us. I don't lose hope of covering the entire planet with love and healing it from so much pain. Let's start with ourselves and we'll surely see the day when, as in my dream, we'll see that paradise on Earth. Meanwhile, follow the voice of your heart, follow it when it tells you to leave everything behind that ties you down and makes you dirty so that you can feel free and light and go through life feeding hearts with your peace.

<u>Practical exercise</u>

Look for the place you consider sacred, a place you have designated for meditation, reflection, prayer and inner observation. Sit here or lie down and make yourself comfortable. Breathe deeply, beginning to be aware of your breathing, until you notice that it's calm and deep. Now I want you to imagine that a golden light from your heart covers your entire body. Now it covers your surroundings, the house, and goes beyond to cover your block, your neighborhood, your city and now your country. I want you to imagine how this light connects with the light of other hearts vibrating like you, I want you to feel the power of this light, a power so great that it can heal you and heal others. Now that light covers the entire planet and goes beyond this galaxy to the ends of the universe. Stay there for a while enjoying this greatness, your greatness. Smile, give thanks for being part of this great universal love. Now gradually see the light reversing its expansion until it comes back into your chest. Put your hands on your heart, give thanks once again and place this light in your hands. I want you to feel this strength in your hands, so that from now on, whenever you need that light, you know that it is as close as the palm of your hand.

<u>Tips</u>

- Look for a globe and heart stickers. Now, put a sticker on that place in the world where we know there's a need for more love, and put the intention in your heart to send love to that part of the planet.
- Look for a heart of rose quartz and when you need to feed on this love, place this quartz in the sunlight and let it bathe in its rays. On the days you feel weak or downcast, put this heart near your bedside table, your wallet or under your pillow to remind you that you're part of that great universal love.

Diary

Write down ways to show your love for the planet: recycle, donate your time to a charity, etc. Everything counts, believe me. Your energy, strength and will are needed, and your presence is valued. Everything you want to do or are doing has a great impact on the future of our planet. You're more important than you know!

____

____

____

____

____

____

____

____

____

____

____

____

Chapter 10: Living in Peace

"May the light illumine your path now and forever. May the darkness never overshadow your heart. Your heart is there to strengthen the good in you."

Peace will be born as a result of putting these little exercises into practice. Feed your essence, keep your heart clean and practice universal love every day. Peace is a tenant in healthy bodies and quiet minds. Have you ever known a criminal to live in peace? Surely not. Peace is added to you as the blessings that will begin to flow in your life once you love universally and flow freely in the universe. The divine thing about being at peace is that, like love, it bears fruit. Love and peace are actually allies, hence the famous phrase: "Peace and love."

This little book was written as a manual since I wanted it to be practical. The idea is that people who need its light can go to it in the middle of a storm and find more than a book—an ally and a friend. I want you to know that this book, despite being relatively short, was stored in my computer for a long time. As I learned things, I added details to it, and I waited to publish it until I considered it was ready. I thought, "Who am I to talk about peace and forgiveness if I don't fully embrace those feelings in my heart myself?" It took me a couple of years, a deep inner cleansing process, to get to where I am now and finally publish this book with the total freedom to tell everyone that every single word is part of my life and my happiness. Peace, my dear friends, is the most precious treasure I possess. It is worth going through our own storms, facing all our fears, the past and the uncertainties, to feel that peace that covers everything with love.

I want to end this book by telling you a great truth: we all have God's peace imprinted on our souls. When we don't know it, when we turn away from this great truth, everything goes wrong like when a child turns away from his family and begins to have difficulties. In the same way, I know that we're all unique and different, and yet everything flows from the same source. That source is LOVE. Embrace that truth with your new clean heart and wrap your whole life in that divine grace that will not only protect you but will bring you the greatest happiness in the world. You were born to smile. You were born to be a hero of love.

When night falls and you see the first star that catches your eye, I want you to thank it for its light. That star was the one who inspired me to write this book. Thank you for letting me accompany you on this adventure, thank you for reading.

Never forget that everything you seek on the outside is within you: that great love and peace that you yearn for, so earnestly. We attract into our lives what we really are. There is no doubt in my heart that you're a source of light, peace and love.

<u>Practical exercise</u>

This exercise is somewhat advanced, but I have absolute faith that if you have done the other meditations, you'll be able to do this one without any problem.

During the week, on the most stressful day in the office or at the university, I want you to disconnect for a few seconds from your surroundings and close your eyes. Just a few seconds. Here, take a deep breath and say to yourself: "I am peace." You'll notice that when you open your eyes, everything will keep on going rapidly but you'll be more calm, aware now that you're an instrument of peace.

Once again, it should be stressed that peace is not something that is achieved or obtained. Like love, peace is always there! We have to be aware of its existence in order to break down all the barriers that keep us from it.

<u>Tips</u>

- Print out a photo of yourself where you're at ease, in nature: on the beach, at a lake or in a park. If you don't have a picture of yourself, look for a magazine cut-out.

- Keep this picture close to the area where you usually get stressed. Remember at all times that this is your reality, your essence. We often confuse sporadic moments with our reality.

- Who are you? You're not what you do, and you're not what you have. When you feel lost from your axis, look at these images that take you back to your origin, to your paradise.

The important thing is to remember, through these images, is that the goal is to live in peace, without letting external sources divert us from our purpose on Earth: to be happy, to love and to be at peace.

<u>**Diary**</u>

Describe the most beautiful scenes of your life, where you felt you were living in a dream come true. I want you to look at the details, what you were saying, how you were feeling. Pay attention and notice that all these scenes had something in common. What was it? Did you discover it? I'll bet you that you felt it somehow in all of them. The secret is to replicate this emotion because we attract what we feel.

____

____

____

____

____

____

____

____

____

____

Thanks

Special thanks to all my friends in heaven. Thank you, wonderful daughter, for blessing my life with your presence. Thank you, my two boys, for teaching me about unconditional love. Thanks to my husband, for being my earthly angel. Without you, Laura Orvieto would not exist.

Thank you, dear reader, for helping me accomplish my mission. These words were written especially for you.

May love and peace live in your life and soul forever.

Laura Orvieto